I cannot leave. Men do not abandon their ships, and women do not abandon their children.
August 27, 1937

THE LANTERN BEARERS SERIES

When the night is darkest, there are always those who hold up a lantern to light the way.

Book 1: The Lamp of Education

The Winter Plum: How Wu Yifang Became the First Woman to Sign the UN Charter

From bound feet in 1893 China to the United Nations in 1945, Wu Yifang bloomed like a winter plum—fearless in frost, fragrant and strong. She became China's first female PhD in Biology, led Ginling College through World War II, and became the first woman to sign the UN Charter. Her lamp of education lit the way for generations.

Book 2: The Lamp of Compassion

The Sheltering Tree: How Minnie Vautrin Saved 10,000 Lives in Wartime China

When darkness fell on Nanjing in 1937, Minnie Vautrin became a sheltering tree, her branches wide enough to protect ten thousand women and children. The "Goddess of Nanking" stood between soldiers and refugees, risking her life daily. Her lamp of compassion burned through the darkest nights.

Book 3: The Lamp of Truth

The Iris Blooms: How Iris Chang Revealed the Truth About the Nanjing Massacre

Like the iris flower—her namesake—Iris Chang bloomed in defiance, revealing truths the world had forgotten. Her groundbreaking book *The Rape of Nanking* (1997) broke sixty years of silence and awakened global awareness. Her lamp of truth continues to shine, reminding us that memory is an act of justice.

Three women. Three flowers. Three lamps. Together, they prove that even a single flame can drive away the darkness.
May their light inspire you to be brave, to be kind, and to stand for truth.

The Sheltering Tree

How Minnie Vautrin Saved 10,000 Lives in Wartime China

Written by
TAN FENGXIA

Illustrated by
LIU JIUMING

Books Beyond Boundaries
ROYAL COLLINS

The Sheltering Tree: How Minnie Vautrin Saved 10,000 Lives in Wartime China

Book 2 of *The Lantern Bearers Series*

Writer: Tan Fengxia
Acquisitions editor: Yu Xiaohua
Illustrator: Liu Jiuming
Translator: Wu Bolin

First published in 2026 by Royal Collins Publishing Group Inc.
Groupe Publication Royal Collins Inc.
550-555 boul. René-Lévesque O Montréal (Québec) H2Z1B1 Canada

10 9 8 7 6 5 4 3 2 1

Originally published in Chinese as《仁爱之灯：魏特琳的故事》

ISBN: 978-1-4878-1388-8

To find out more about our publications, please visit www.royalcollins.com.

"I cannot leave. Men do not abandon their ships,
and women do not abandon their children."

—MINNIE VAUTRIN, 1937

Summer in Secor, Illinois. Cornfields stretched endlessly. Young Minnie Vautrin ran with her brother. “I want to grow strong,” she thought, “like corn—tall and sturdy.”

But shadows fell early. Her mother passed away when Minnie was six. Overnight, she became the little adult—plowing fields, scrubbing laundry, cooking meals.

Her only comfort was the garden, watering the roses her mother had planted.

Minnie was tough, but she was brilliant.

She dreamed of being a teacher, but her father said no. "We are poor, and girls do not need education."

Minnie fought for her future. She took every odd job, saving for tuition. She worked her way through the University of Illinois, graduating with honors.

Her heart was big enough for more than her hometown.

Autumn 1912. A new horizon called. Minnie said goodbye to her family and the cornfields. She boarded a steamship bound for China.

振興中華
永和興

China was a land of ancient walls and new struggles. Minnie arrived in Hefei, where children waited to grow. She gave herself a Chinese name: Hua Qun (华群, Serving the Group). She was ready to serve.

In Hefei, she became the principal of San Yu Girls' School.

People said, "A woman's virtue is having no talent."

"No!" Hua Qun replied. "Education changes destiny."

She filled the schoolyard with seeds. When autumn came, golden chrysanthemums burst into bloom. "You have the right to bloom," she told her students. "Just like these flowers."

For six years, she worked with prairie-storm energy.

In 1918, she returned to America for rest. Her heart drifted back across the ocean.

A shopkeeper offered her a gift. Minnie chose a sturdy umbrella. “I will need this in China,” she smiled.

This umbrella would soon become a shield for thousands.

1919. A new door opened.

Minnie joined Ginling College—China’s first university for women. She stepped onto campus, umbrella in hand. Students lined up to welcome her.

Ginling was no longer just a school. It was her sanctuary. It was her home.

Minnie became Dean of Education at Ginling College, occasionally serving as Acting President.

She revolutionized teaching in China. She didn't just lecture—she established a student-teaching system, sending her girls out to practice. She was training the teachers who would shape China's future.

She also built a home for them.

Minnie led the planning of the new campus, planting trees and flowers with her own hands. Every autumn, she held a Chrysanthemum Show. Golden blooms filled the courtyard, fearless of frost.

President Wu Yifang smiled at her: "Minnie, your love for chrysanthemums rivals the ancient Chinese poets!" Minnie laughed.

Minnie refused to stay inside the ivory tower. She shared her beloved flowers with neighbors outside the walls.

On weekends, she rode her bicycle through narrow alleys, visiting families in need. She urged her students: "Go out. Serve the people. Understand their hardships."

They turned words into action. They opened a primary school for poor children. They taught hygiene and treated the sick.

For girls who had no school, Minnie opened home economics classes. The neighbors loved the tall American woman. They brought her their best food and called her "Miss Hua."

She was family.

Minnie worked hard, but she climbed harder.

She led students up Mount Tai's thousands of steps. "Keep going! Victory is ahead!" she shouted, striding in front like a general.

She taught them: To climb life's mountains—a woman needs a strong mind and a strong body.

She never forgot her graduates.

One freezing night, she trekked through a blizzard to find a student's home. When she appeared—covered in snow, holding a lantern and a gift—the student wept with joy.

Minnie smiled. She had traveled far to see her seeds blooming.

Ginling became her true home. She traveled back to America twice, not to rest, but to raise money and recruit teachers, determined to give Chinese women a world-class education.

It was the mission of her life, day and night.

But devotion came with a cost.

Letters arrived from Illinois: her father was aging; he needed her. Minnie sat by her window, watching the snow fall. Her heart was torn between two duties.

In the end, she chose Ginling. She would carry this ache forever.

Happy
50th
Birthday!

1936. The gardener turned fifty.

She refused a party, but she couldn't stop her students' love. They surprised her with a play called *The Ginling Toy Shop*. When the final doll appeared—exactly fifty years old—Minnie laughed until she cried.

She had no children of her own, yet she was mother to them all.

But the laughter was silenced by a scream from the sky.

Summer 1937. The dark net of war fell over China. Japanese warplanes dove on Nanjing. Boom! Ancient towers crumbled. Smoke choked the sun.

In the rubble, a pot of chrysanthemums lay overturned—golden petals spilled into dust, crushed by the storm of war.

"Run to the shelters!" When sirens wailed, Minnie didn't run away—she ran toward the frightened. She grabbed the hand of a terrified child and led him into the earth.

Outside, moonlight was shattered by fire. Inside the dark cave, they huddled around a single lantern. The flowers left behind shut tight—like little clenched fists, silent and angry.

War closed in. Train stations were filled with panic. People scrambled onto trains, desperate to escape. "Will the Japanese come?" Neighbors grabbed Minnie's hands, eyes full of fear. "When will this end?" While others packed to flee, Minnie unpacked her heart. She decided she would not run.

By day, she held the brokenhearted. By night, she wrote by candlelight, her pen scratching against distant cannons.

She asked the darkness: "Would that the moral forces of the world could be mobilized against war ..."

But the world was silent.

The school could not open. The city was emptying. The American Embassy ordered: "Evacuate. It is too dangerous."

President Wu Yifang gave the teachers a choice.

Minnie's answer was written in stone. "I cannot leave. Men do not abandon their ships. Women do not abandon their children."

October 1937. The cannons roared, but the gardeners still put out the chrysanthemums. The flowers bloomed in cold wind, fearless and proud.

"Righteousness will triumph," Minnie whispered.

It was time to say goodbye. President Wu would lead students west. Minnie would guard the campus. Two branches of the same tree.

The enemy closed in. Minnie didn't wait.

She joined the International Safety Zone Committee. She threw open the gates of Ginling College. "This is a sanctuary," she declared.

Classrooms became bedrooms. Desks became beds. She prepared to shelter those who had nowhere left to run.

December 13, 1937. The city fell. The Massacre began.

Darkness swallowed Nanjing's streets. But inside Ginling, a light still burned.

Minnie walked the halls with her lantern, checking on terrified women hiding in basements and attics. She was the watcher in the night.

Japanese soldiers came burning and killing without mercy. They had no shame, no law. They ignored the Safety Zone completely.

Like bandits, they broke in from everywhere—scaling walls, kicking down gates, hunting to seize and drag away the defenseless.

Minnie became a sentinel, running from gate to gate, courtyard to courtyard, blocking their path again and again.

When a soldier grabbed a girl, Minnie threw herself between them. She spread her arms. "Stop!" she commanded.

He slapped her face. He thrust his bayonet at her. He aimed his pistol at her heart. She did not flinch.

"This is my home. You shall not pass."

Winter bit deep. Refugees shivered in thin rags.

Minnie and her team handed out cotton quilts and hot gruel. When the pot was empty, she gave her own bowl to a latecomer. “Eat,” she said gently.

But her voice to the crowd was iron-strong: “China has not fallen! We will not fall!”

War destroys buildings, but it must not destroy a nation's spine.

At the school gate, Minnie saw a boy wearing an armband with the Japanese rising sun—a badge of submission to stay safe. She held his hand gently, her eyes stern but kind.

"You do not need this. You are Chinese. Never forget who you are." She removed the badge. The boy nodded, tears in his eyes.

Resistance wasn't just guns—it was daily life.

Minnie refused to ride Japanese buses. She took Chinese rickshaws, ensuring her neighbors earned the fare.

Passing the fields, she saw farmers tilling scorched earth, planting new seeds. She smiled at their resilience. "Nothing can stop the crops from rising again."

Spring returned. War could destroy walls, but it could not stop the flowers.

Minnie brought roses from the park to plant in scarred earth. Under moonlight, she knelt in the dirt, digging life back into the garden.

She wrote: "The roses make us glad ... but under this beautiful moon, the bombers will come." She planted anyway. To plant a garden is to believe in tomorrow.

She fought the darkness with light—the light of education.

She opened classes for the women, teaching them to knit and sew, to earn their own bread. She opened a nursery for the children. “Stand up,” she told them. “Be strong. Be useful.”

Using her own savings, she bought land for a school. Amid the ruins, the sound of reading rose again.

She bought quilts for freezing neighbors. She gave away every coin she had.

One day, two boys watched her pass on her bicycle. "Look! A foreign lady!" the little one cried. "Hush!" his brother scolded. "That is Miss Hua. Grandma calls her the 'Goddess.' She protects us."

She was no longer American. She belonged to Nanjing.

The Japanese ordered, "Close the camp." But many women had no home, or home meant danger. Minnie defied the command. "The gates stay open," she declared.

Women knelt before her, tears streaming. "Our Goddess," they whispered, "our guardian angel."

"No, no." Minnie helped them stand. "I have not done enough. This success is all of us, working together. United in heart, China will not fall!"

May 14, 1940. The gardener had given everything. The nightmare of war had exhausted her body and broken her spirit. She had to go home to heal.

Standing on the deck, she looked back at the receding shore. The vast ocean mirrored her tears. She had served China for twenty-eight years.

"Farewell, my beloved Nanjing. If I had a second life, I would give it to you again. For China ... China is my home."

A year later, on May 14, 1941, Minnie Vautrin passed away in America.

But her spirit returned to Nanjing.

Her headstone was carved in the shape of a Chinese roof. Under the eaves, four characters are etched in traditional style, reading from right to left:

永生金陵 (Forever Ginling)

Words to Know

Hua Qun
Minnie's Chinese name means "Serving the Group." The character *hua* means "splendid" or "Chinese," while *qun* means "crowd" or "group."

Ginling College
The first college in China to grant bachelor's degrees to women. Wu Yifang was its president, and Minnie Vautrin served as Dean of Education.

Nanjing (Nanking)
The capital city of China during World War II.

International Safety Zone
A designated area in Nanjing where foreigners tried to protect Chinese civilians from the Japanese army during the Nanjing Massacre.

Nanjing Massacre
A tragic event (1937–1938) during World War II, when many innocent people in Nanjing suffered. Minnie Vautrin and others worked to protect survivors.

"Goddess of Nanking"
A name given to Minnie by refugees because she saved their lives like a guardian angel.

Chrysanthemum
A flower that blooms in autumn. In Chinese culture, it represents resilience and strength in the face of cold.

The Journey of Minnie Vautrin (1886–1941)

The Goddess of Nanking

1886	Born on September 27 in Secor, Illinois.
1912	Graduated from the University of Illinois. Sailed to China to serve as Principal of San Yu Girls' School in Hefei.
1919	Joined Ginling College in Nanjing as Dean of Education. Revolutionized teacher training in China.
1937	World War II reached Nanjing. Minnie refused to evacuate, helping establish the International Safety Zone.
December 1937	During the Nanjing Massacre, transformed Ginling College into a sanctuary, saving more than 10,000 women and children.
1940	Suffering from severe trauma and exhaustion, returned to the US on May 14.
1941	Passed away on May 14. Buried in Shepherd, Michigan.
2023	On April 12, a monument to Minnie was unveiled in Secor, Illinois. The state proclaimed: "Minnie Vautrin Day."

Selected Bibliography

Hu, Hua-Ling. *American Goddess at the Rape of Nanking: The Courage of Minnie Vautrin*. Carbondale: Southern Illinois University Press, 2000.

Vautrin, Minnie. *The Diary of Minnie Vautrin*. Translated by Nanjing Massacre Research Center. Nanjing: Jiangsu People's Publishing House, 2000.

Zhang, Lianhong, ed. *Eternal Ginling: A Biography of Minnie Vautrin*. Nanjing: Nanjing Publishing House, 2024.

About the Author

TAN FENGXIA is a Hans Christian Andersen Award Juror (2024, 2026) and Professor of Children's Literature at Nanjing Normal University, China.

As one of the world's leading scholars of children's books, she has devoted her career to bringing Chinese stories to young readers everywhere. She has been a research fellow at Cambridge University and the International Youth Library in Munich.

The Sheltering Tree is her tribute to the brave women of Nanjing—the city where she has lived and taught for decades, walking the same paths Minnie Vautrin once walked.

Tan Fengxia believes every child deserves to see themselves as a hero of history.

I love Jinling deeply.
Had I ten lives, I would
give them all to her... May
those who are determined to
devote their strength to this
cause, find the vision to go
forward.
May 14, 1941

About the Illustrator

LIU JIUMING is a distinguished artist and faculty member in the Illustration Department at Nanjing University of the Arts. He is a member of the China Artists Association and the Jiangsu Artists Association.

For *The Sheltering Tree*, he uses a striking woodcut style to capture the weight of history and the resilience of life. His powerful artwork has been selected for China's most prestigious exhibitions.

His works are held in the National Art Museum of China, the Jiangsu Art Museum, and other distinguished collections.